one step closer

one step closer

A Guided Tour of the Spiritual Life

David Edwards

Our purpose at Howard Publishing is to:

- *Increase faith* in the hearts of growing Christians
- *Inspire holiness* in the lives of believers
- *Instill hope* in the hearts of struggling people everywhere

Because He's coming again!

One Step Closer © 1999 by David Edwards
All rights reserved. Printed in the United States of America

Published by Howard Publishing Co., Inc.,
3117 North 7th Street, West Monroe, LA 71291-2227

99 00 01 02 03 04 05 06 07 08 10 9 8 7 6 5 4 3 2 1

Compiled by LeAnn Weiss
Interior Design by Stephanie Denney
Cover Design by LinDee Loveland

Library of Congress Cataloging-in-Publication Data
Edwards, David, date.
    One step closer / David Edwards.
        p. cm.
    ISBN 1-58229-002-4
    1. Meditations. 2. Young adults--Prayer-books and devotions-
-English. I. Title.
BV4850.E35 1998   98-20678
248.8'4--dc21   CIP

CONTENTS

"**Thanks be to God for His indescribable gift.**"

—2 Corinthians 9:15

"You are our letter, written in our hearts, known and read by all men." —2 Corinthians 3:2

Thank you

Flingie
Feni
LeAnn
LinDee
Howard Publishing
R. H.

Meet David Edwards

David Edwards travels the country full time, speaking to young adults in churches and a variety of other settings. A native of Oklahoma City, Oklahoma, David holds a Bachelor of Arts degree in religion from Oklahoma City University. He has also completed graduate work toward a Master of Divinity.

A gifted communicator, David speaks from his heart about issues relevant to Generation X.

David has been a featured speaker for City-Wide Weekly Bible Study Groups in Texas, Oklahoma, Alabama, Arkansas, Mississippi, Louisiana, Georgia, and Florida.

David is the author of the *Destinations* video series and the "How to Make Life All Good" witnessing tract.

David has a heart for young adults. A member of Generation X himself, David knows firsthand the world of this generation. He helps them discover the importance of a Christ-centered lifestyle. David masterfully applies biblical truths to the current issues of the day in an honest, humorous and understandable form.

David's mission is to reintroduce the truth of God's Word by meeting people where they are in life and bringing them one step closer to knowing and becoming like Jesus Christ.

Introduction

Christianity is not a one-time event...it's ongoing and ever changing. In short, Christianity is the process by which we are made into the image of Christ. God's role in this process is that He meets you wherever you are in life and, through time, brings you one step closer to Him. This book is designed to help you in that process. It's not just a book to be read, it's a book to be used.

You'll notice that the chapter titles in the book all contain verbs or action words. These action words are "our roles" in getting closer to God. For example, chapter 2 is titled "Trusting God with the Details." That's our role—it's our job to trust, not God's. I suggest that you look at each chapter title as a *step*—a step toward a deeper relationship with God.

Within each chapter, you will find quotes and questions to help you think, principles to practice daily in your walk, verses to encourage you and build you up, prayers to guide your thoughts and heart, steps to action, and along the journey breakpoints to move you into deeper commitment. My prayer for you is that this book will help you to stay focused, to stay faithful, and to bring you one step closer.

one step closer

_____
(insert your name)

Your **steps** are established by Me. I delight in your way. Even though you may stumble, **you will not fall, for I am the One who holds your hand.**

—Psalm 37:23–24, paraphrase

Taking Steps toward Relationship with Him

All of the Christian life is built around a relationship with Jesus Christ. That relationship is a process that takes us one step closer to Him. We are never alone. He takes each step with us. His agenda is to make us better than ever. He wants to make our lives all good.

I spoke once at a juvenile detention center. While I was there, this guy came up to me and said that he liked my talk about the choices we make in life. I asked him, "What is life about?" He said, "Freedom man. It's all about freedom. You do what you want to do."

To which I said, "You know what blows my mind the most? When I'm done here, I'm the one who gets to leave."

The things in our world that promise freedom and individual rights, in reality imprison and restrict us. The enemy entices us with choices that seem harmless. He paints the Christian life as God's attempt to pull the plug on the party and keep us from the pursuit of happiness and all the prizes that go with the American Dream.

But the truth is that real freedom comes only from a personal relationship with Jesus Christ and following Him. He created us, and only He knows what will bring us true fulfillment. He knows that everything else leads us to futile, fruitless emptiness and hollow dreams.

_____ ,
(insert your name)

I loved you so much that I sent My one and only Son, Jesus, to die in your place. Just believe in His Name and you will have life. You'll live forever with Me!

— John 3:16, paraphrase

Sin separates you from God.

No amount of money, success, or ability can fix that. Nobody is born a Christian.

For by grace you have been saved through faith; and that not of yourselves, it is the gift of God; not as a result of works, that no one should boast.

—Ephesians 2:8–9

2

Sin is not just something we do...**it's a condition** that makes us do stupid things. We're born with it. But God demonstrates His own love toward us, in that while we were yet sinners, Christ died for us.

—Romans 5:8

If you were to go to a costume party, what would you dress up as?

_____

_____

We all have masks that keep people from seeing the real us. What mask do you wear most often?

_____

_____

God can see right through it!

Christianity is not God's attempt to limit us but to get us out of self-destructive ways.

Think of a time when something seemed like a good idea at the time, but it actually wasn't._____
_____
_____

There is a way which seems right to a man, but its end is the way of death.

—Proverbs 14:12

3

Until we're real with God, God can't be real with us.

Whoever will call
upon the name of
the Lord will
be saved.

—Romans 10:13

But as many as received Him,
to them He gave the right to
become children of God,
even to those who believe
in His name.

—John 1:12

All of our best efforts can't get us into God's presence.

Only God can make us clean!

And again a voice came to him a second time, "What God has cleansed, no longer consider unholy." —Acts 10:15

Recall a time when you went out of your way to please somebody or to win someone's affection, and it didn't work.

Jesus said to him, "I am the **WAY**, and the **TRUTH**, and the **LIFE**; no one comes to the Father, but through Me." —John 14:6

5

Photo by Greg Howell

God moves heaven and

If we confess our sins, He is faithful and righteous

earth for anyone who asks.

to forgive us our sins and to cleanse us from all

When we make the choice,

unrighteousness. —1 John 1:9

God makes the change!

Along the Journey

Have you solved the problem of separation between you and God? If you were to stand before Jesus today, would He know you by name? Describe your relationship with God in one sentence.

_____

_____

_____

_____

The **first** critical **step** toward a relationship with God is **trusting** Jesus Christ to be the leader of your life.

If you could send only one e-mail to all your friends about your **belief in God,** what would it say?_____

_____
_____
_____
_____
_____
_____
_____
_____
_____
_____

Get God into your life!!!

one 1. Recognize you are separated from God.

two 2. Be willing to turn toward God.

three 3. Believe that Jesus Christ died for you on the Cross and beat death.

four 4. Invite Jesus Christ to come in and be the leader of your life.

Dear God,
I know my sin has separated me from You. I believe You sent Jesus to die for me. I ask You to forgive me. I now turn my life over to You and receive Jesus as the leader of my heart and life. In Jesus' name, Amen.

If you've already asked Jesus to be the leader of your life, take time to **thank God** for the **difference He has made** in your life. What is the single most valuable thing God has ever taught you?

Only fear the Lord and serve Him in truth with all your heart; for consider what great things He has done for you.

—1 Samuel 12:24

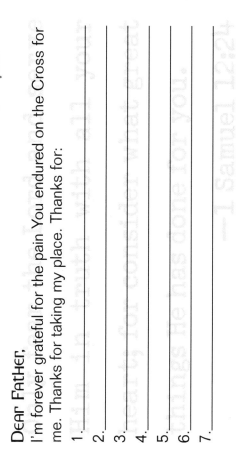

Dear Father,

I'm forever grateful for the pain You endured on the Cross for me. Thanks for taking my place. Thanks for:

1. _____

2. _____

3. _____

4. _____

5. _____

6. _____

7. _____

—1 Samuel 12:24

prayer

Think of some friends or people you know who haven't yet asked God to step out of heaven and into their lives. Commit to pray for them and to ask God to give you divine opportunities to share Him with them.

Lord,

Give me creative ways to share with the following people how You have made my life all good. They need You to become the leader of their hearts and lives.

1._____

2._____

3._____

Trusting God with the Details

Ever go into a movie with people who talked during the whole thing? You know...by day they seem like nice people. They're your friends. But when the lights go out, they begin to talk and talk and talk. Irritating, isn't it? I've found that there are two kinds of movie talkers. There are those who ask, "Why is this happening?" or "What is going on?" I always want to say, "Did I get here before you? Shh. Be quiet." Then there are those who have to yell out the next scene before it actually occurs. "Yeah, thanks a lot Sherlock, I guess I can go back to coloring now that I don't have to watch the rest of the movie—since you have it all figured out for me."

I think that people are like that because they don't like surprises. They want to have the whole thing figured out beforehand. Some of us are like that spiritually too. We trust God with what we're comfortable with—the areas whose outcomes we already know. But the secret of the Christian life is trusting God with all the details and letting the details rest in His silent control. We have to let God run the show. Often, you'll find that the Christian life demands that we trust Him *without* knowing the outcome. For this is the very nature of trust.

Our relationship with Jesus becomes the compass by which we make all decisions. The question is, "What does God want?"

But seek first His kingdom and His righteousness; and all these things shall be added to you.
—Matthew 6:33

God sends us into storms to shape our security. He wants us to depend on Him alone.

Because he has loved Me, therefore I will deliver him; I will set him securely on high, because he has known My name. He will call upon Me, and I will answer him; I will be with him in trouble; I will rescue him, and honor him. —Psalm 91:14-15

What is your **worst** fear? ....
....
....
....

WHAT does God's Word say about it?
....
....
....
....

12

Read Mark 4:35–36. If you were a meteorologist, what would be the forecast of your next storm?......................................
....
....

Ask Jesus to calm the storms in your life and permit Him to speak direction to your life. • Sometimes God wants you to give up the good things. He wants you to trust Him so that your life is in **COOPERATION** with His will. You can't live in opposition to God and know His will. • **Check out Proverbs 3:1–12.**

along the   journey

Ask God to reveal if there are any good things in your life that He wants you to give to Him as an act of trust. Are you looking to Him in everything you do? Are you choosing God's best over what you think is best? • I will instruct you and teach you in the way which you should go; I will counsel you with My eye upon you. Do not be as the horse or as the mule which have no understanding, whose trappings include bit and bridle to hold them in check, otherwise they will not come near to you. [Don't let your stubbornness keep you from obeying God.] Many are the sorrows of the wicked; but he who trusts in the Lord, lovingkindness shall surround him. —Psalm 32:8–10

13

What terrifies you the most

. . . .

greater

Sometimes when God doesn't appear to come through, it's because He's preparing you for something **greater** than what you're wanting.

When you go through a time of doubt, good theology will pull you through. **You fight doubt with good theology.**

For whatever was written in earlier times was written for our instruction, that through perseverance and the encouragement of the Scriptures we might have hope. —Romans 15:4

14

If it be so, our God whom we serve is able to deliver us from the furnace of blazing fire; and He will deliver us out of your hand, O king. But even if He does not, let it be known to you, O king, that we are not going to serve your gods or worship the golden image that you have set up.
—Daniel 3:17–18

In the darkest moments when you're faced with doubt, you must stare at doubt and say, "You can't have me!"

Immediately the boy's father cried out and began saying, "I do believe; help my unbelief." —Mark 9:24

If you could ask God to do one thing in your lifetime, what would it be? ....
....
....

Remember, God wants us to seek His face...not just the provisions of His hands. Are you looking to God for who He is and not just what He can do for you?

Read Mark 8

There will be situations when it will be difficult to trust God. But when you trust in God, you will never be disappointed!

Behold, I lay in Zion a stone of stumbling and a rock of offense, and he who believes in Him will not be disappointed. —Romans 9:33

16

thought...

How do you know when it's God?

    1. The timing is right!

        2. Trust is required.

            3. You will see tremendous results!

"It is the Lord." And so when Simon Peter heard that it was the Lord, he put his outer garment on (for he was stripped for work), and threw himself into the sea.
—John 21:7

Don't get distracted with asking *why?* Instead,

> **And we know that God causes all things to work**

ask *who?* **Trusting God** and His sovereignty

> **together for good to those who love God, to those who**

is the key solution to the *why*s of your life.

> **are called according to His purpose. —Romans 8:28**

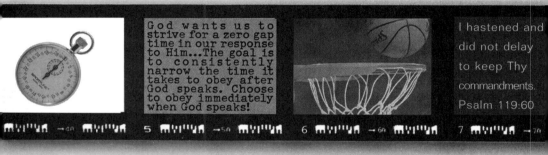

God wants us to strive for a zero gap time in our response to Him...The goal is to consistently narrow the time it takes to obey after God speaks. Choose to obey immediately when God speaks!

I hastened and did not delay to keep Thy commandments. Psalm 119:60

along the journey

What is it that He has told you to do that you haven't done yet? . .
. . . . .Get on with it!

What one thing could your friends or family do to assure that you

would never speak to them again? . . . .

Now let it go!!!

Make a decision to obey God and to act upon what He had asked you to do now.

The enemy wants us to become preoccupied with what isn't in our lives. Have you believed any of his lies by thinking, "If only I had . . . .($$$, the right person to love me, the dream job, success, better friends, more time, etc.), I would be happy? If God leaves a need unmet, it's because He wants you to trust Him as your . . . .

Don't **waste** your time

...worrying doesn't fix or change anything. It just makes you a nervous wreck. The key is remembering who is in control and giving your worries to Him.

Read Matthew 6:25–33

When you feel overwhelmed and at the end of your rope, look

Worry is just trying to solve problems our way,

up and remember...Your help comes from the Lord, the maker

without factoring in the Presence of God!

of heaven and earth! — Psalm 121:1–2, paraphrase

Father,

help me to trust You with all the details of my life. I want You to call all the shots, even if I don't see the wisdom of Your plan at the time. Help me to willingly give You all the pieces to the puzzle of my life, trusting that You are going to guide each step as I seek to acknowledge You in all I say and do. I know you see the entire picture and love me enough to lead me in the paths that are best for me. Help me to leave the outcome to You. Thanks for Your faithfulness!

I will bless the Lord who has counseled me; indeed, my mind instructs me in the night. I have set the Lord continually before me; because He is at my right hand, I will not be shaken. Therefore my heart is glad, and my glory rejoices; my flesh also will dwell securely. For Thou wilt not abandon my soul to Sheol; neither wilt Thou allow Thy Holy One to see the pit. Thou wilt make known to me the path of life; in Thy presence is fullness of joy; in Thy right hand there are pleasures forever.

—Psalm 16:7–11

20

Obtaining Freedom from the Past

For a season in my life, I traveled with a married friend of mine who had a little baby boy who was just learning to walk. We heard frequent progress reports during our road trips. Over the phone his wife would share how their baby tried to take a step and instead awkwardly crashed into the furniture or floor in each valiant attempt.

But there came that day when his son took **His first step**—and he didn't fall over. He stayed up! I promise you that my friend's wife didn't call him to say, "Your son, Chad, fell one hundred forty-nine times today before taking one little step. I counted every fall—what an idiot. He must take after your side of the family!" Instead, she called to excitedly report, "He did it! He took his first step and he made it!"

God doesn't count our falls. He doesn't say, "Do you believe it? That's the hundredth time Henry has lied this month," or "For heaven's sake, that's the one-thousandth and first time Karen has gossiped this year." You won't hear our heavenly Father saying, "Forget it, there's no hope for Harry—he's on his eighth affair and third marriage; I can't possibly use him now!"

When you blow it, repent and turn to God. Your best days are still in front of you. God completely forgets your falls. He truly forgives and forgets by taking your sins and casting them as far as the east is from the west. And He's always there to cheer you on with each little step you make on your journey in becoming a fully devoted follower of Jesus Christ.

Sin is sin! In God's eyes, one sin isn't worse than another. But if God did have a "Top Ten" list of sins, surely something as bad as an adultery/murder combination would be somewhere near the top of that list.

Most of us are familiar with King David's adulterous affair with Bathsheba and his ultimate murder of her husband in an attempt to cover up their steamy affair. But what did David, "a man after God's own heart," do after he had majorly blown it?

If you could be forgiven of only one sin, what would it be? _____

Read 2 Samuel 12:20 to look at God's blueprint for restoration after David's sin with Bathsheba.

When you ask God to forgive you, be confident that there is no condemnation because you are in Christ Jesus. Thank God that you've been set free from the law of sin and death!

Memorize
Romans 8:1-2

King David's Steps toward GOD after Blowing It!

1 He **admitted** to God that he was wrong.
Father, I blew it. What I did was wrong. I don't have any excuses. I know it broke Your heart. Please forgive me. I'm so sorry for_____
_____.

2 He **understood** that God distinguished between who he was and what he'd done.
Father, thanks that nothing I've done can change Your unconditional love for me! Lord, help me to allow You to begin Your cleaning process in my life. I want to cooperate with Your restoration in my life.

3 He **realized** he had been wrong, and he moved back toward God knowing that God still loved and accepted him unconditionally—faults and all.

4 He **believed** that God had totally forgiven him and still had good plans for him.

5 David **continued** on in his position as king and did even greater things after he had been restored by God.

23

Think of a time in your life when you blew it—and you're still dealing with it. Use David's steps to put the past in the past so you can move forward.

What is the biggest mistake you have ever made in your life?

_____

Don't bother writing it out;

It **has** been **forgiven!**

Photo by Greg Howell

The enemy wants to constantly remind you of your past mistakes in order to trick you into feeling so unworthy that you won't take part in the exciting ways God wants to work through your life. God never brings up your past to beat you up or to remind you how you blew it! God deals with your past to set you free. If your past has driven you back into the presence of God, it has served its purpose!

God is the Great Come-Back King. He takes the broken pieces of our lives and fixes them and makes us useable and right again. We get to continue on in our position in Him!

Come to Me, all who are weary and heavy-laden, and I will give you rest.
—Matthew 11:28

Along the Journey

Are you letting the enemy weigh you down with your past baggage? Are you believing the enemy's lie that you have to settle for God's second best because you fell? What broken pieces do you need to give to The Great Physician to heal?

1.

2.

3.

24

Father,

I'm sorry for _____

_____.

Thanks for covering my mistakes with Your

mercy and grace. When the enemy tries to

rub them in my face, remind me that You don't condemn me or

hold it against me. Thanks for Your ability to take the harmful

things from my past and transform them to work together for my

benefit. I'm forever grateful to You! Thanks for Your commitment

to making me like You. Thanks for Your patience and love

throughout the entire process.

Let him turn away from evil and do good; let him seek peace and pursue it. —1 Peter 3:11

Repent positively!
Every act of Jesus is redemptive.

25

When dealing with the past, God helps us recognize our mistakes.

How many times have you forgiven the people who have hurt you?

Not enough, huh?

us when we obey.

Do not call to mind the former things, or ponder things of the past. Behold, I will do something new, now it will spring forth; will you not be aware of it? I will even make a roadway in the Wilderness, rivers in the desert. —Isaiah 43:18–19

He redirects us where

in His fleshly body through death,

He wants us to go. Then He rewards

We have a choice...We don't have to be chained to our past.

We're forgiven!

He has now reconciled you reproach. —Colossians 1:22

in order to present you before Him

holy and blameless and beyond

Photo by Greg Howell

26

He died for all, that they who live should no

Christianity isn't about doing

longer live for themselves, but for Him who died

stuff. It's not about what you do, it's

and rose again on their behalf.

about what's been done for you.

—2 Corinthians 5:15

God Allows the past to serve as a positive reminder to release the hurts in order that we might move forward.

One thing I do: forgetting what lies behind and reaching forward to what lies ahead, I press on toward the goal for the prize of the upward call of God in Christ Jesus.

—Philippians 3:13–14

God doesn't rub our sin in, He rubbed it out! As far as the east is from the west, so far has He removed our transgressions from us.
—Psalm 103:12

Success doesn't heal the wounds of the past, it deepens them. Only God can heal our wounds.

He took up our infirmities and carried our sorrows, yet we considered him stricken by God, smitten by him, and afflicted.
—Isaiah 53:4 NIV

If you put all of your hurts and regrets into one box, what would go in it and how would you dispose of it?

———————————————————
———————————————————
———————————————————
———————————————————
———————————————————
———————————————————
———————————————————

God is not restricted or regulated by our reactions toward our past. Paul had a past, but God still made him a great man. Are you still letting your fears about the past keep you from your future?

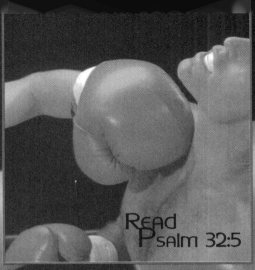

To us, our mistakes are huge. In God's eyes, they're a splinter. **He knocks them right out.** God is much bigger than our mistakes.

Read Psalm 32:5

When Jesus is at the center of our lives, our success makes sense.

JESUS

For I am confident of this very thing, that He who began a good work in you will perfect it until the day of Christ Jesus. —Philippians 1:6

Be thankful that God doesn't deal with or reward us according to our Sin. He has not dealt

with us according to

our sins, nor rewarded

us according to our

iniquities.

—Psalm 103:10

Don't beat yourself up! Once you have confessed, God doesn't want you to keep hanging out in regret and remorse...He calls you to change!

Let the wicked forsake his way, and the unrighteous man his thoughts; and let Him return to the Lord, and He will have compassion on him; and to our God, for He will abundantly pardon.

—Isaiah 55:7

31

Dear God,

I know my tendency is to listen to the regrets of the past. I confess to You that I have given those voices too much power. I turn my back on the past and will no longer allow my attention to be captured by something I can do nothng about.

I see now that my past has brought me to this place where You are working. I commint to do Your will in the challenges of the present. Give me courage and creativity to live in a righteous manner.

You have given me a future and a home. Your plans are for good and not for evil. The future is good because You are good.

Fill my mind and my soul with new plans for the future. Cause a fresh hope to rise in me. This day, I choose to go forward with boldness.

CHAPTER 4

Living in Relationship with Him

I don't know if you drive into the city much, but if you do, you'll see some strange things. For instance, I was driving to a speaking engagement in a very large metropolitan city. I saw this guy wandering down the street talking to himself. I wondered, if you see a guy on one street talking to himself, then you see another guy on a different street talking to himself, are they by some cosmic chance somehow carrying on a conversation with each other??? But, I digress...

I once saw a homeless guy standing at the corner of an intersection with his dog. Let's think about that for a moment—a homeless guy with a dog. I have to ask, what is this dog thinking... "Hey when are we going to get home? This is the longest walk I've ever been on. And besides that, where is my bowl?"

As I thought about that man and his dog, I realized that dog had made one decision. And that decision was to follow his master wherever he led him. He let the master lead no matter how long the journey took or where it led. You don't have to know how your whole life is going to play out. But you do have to decide **who your leader will be.**

Like that old dog—I will live my life following my Master, and I will follow wherever He leads.

Do you not know that your body is a temple of the Holy Spirit who is in you, whom you have from God, and that you are not your own? For you have been bought with a price: therefore glorify God in your body.
—1 Corinthians 6:19–20

The defining quality of the Christian life is the presence of God living in you! **You are God's address!!!**

34

God doesn't ask us
to be perfect—
He just asks us to
be consistent.

He has told you, O man, what is good; and what does the
Lord require of you but to **do justice,** to
love kindness, and to **walk
humbly** with your God? —Micah 6:8

Photo by Greg Howell

The Christian life is not about you doing something for God; it's about God doing something for you and through you.

I am the **vine**, you are the branches; he who abides in Me, and I in him, he bears much fruit; for apart from Me you can do nothing. — John 15:5

What is the most recent thing you've learned about God? _____

_____

_____

_____

_____

_____

The way we express
the presence of Jesus Christ
is by being responsible for what
we've been given and responsive to
the call of God.

As each one has received a
special gift, employ it in serving
one another, as good stewards of the
manifold grace of God.

—1 Peter 4:10

God doesn't want our promises, He **wants our lives.** We can put ourselves in the position to achieve His ultimate freedom by being with Him.

Abide in Me,
and I in you. As the
branch cannot bear fruit of
itself, unless it abides in the
vine, so neither can you,
unless you abide in Me.

—John 15:4

Along the Journey

What is the net that gives you the greatest sense of security?
Relationships, career, family, money, success, etc.? Read Mark 1:16–19.
How could you best serve the Kingdom?_____
_____
Are you willing to drop your net and follow Him?_____
Are you responding immediately when God prompts you?_____

True or False?

> My God fits neatly into the structure of my life.

If you answered true, then your God is too small.
Commit your works to the Lord,
And your plans will be established.
—Proverbs 16:3

Christianity is not about hanging around the cross...it's about **get**ting on it!

If you could **pick one** material possession (religious symbols excluded) to represent your faith, what would it be?_____

For you have **been called** for this purpose, since Christ also **suffered** for you, leaving you an example for you to follow in His steps. —1 Peter 2:21

Our ability to **trust** God with our trials is directly related to our **faith** in His **character**.

Here on earth you will have many trials and sorrows; but **cheer up,** for I have overcome the world.
—John 16:33 LB

Photo by Greg Howell

38

Have you ever come to a point in your life where you've gone from being intrigued with Jesus to **identifying with Him?**

You will be hated by all on account of My name, but it is the one who has endured to the end who will be saved.

—Matthew 10:22

See your walk with the Lord not as paying a price, but as making an INVESTMENT. · He who has found his life shall lose it, and he who has lost his life for My sake shall find it. —Matthew 10:39

Be God's kind of Christian.

But the fruit of the Spirit is love, joy, peace, patience, kindness, goodness, faithfulness, gentleness, self-control; against such things there is no law.

—Galatians 5:22–23

We have to stop living by whatever we want and start living by **whatever God wants.**

What does God want?

Listen to My voice, and **do** according to **all which I command you**; so you shall be My people, and I will be your God. —Jeremiah 11:4

Learning to be content—**wherever** God

But godliness actually is a means of great gain, when

has you—is a key to spiritual growth.

accompanied by contentment. — 1 Timothy 6:6

We're responsible for the presence of God in us, and we're responsible to guard that presence. We can't lose the presence of God in us, but we can quench or smother it. ● And do not grieve the Holy Spirit of God, by whom you were sealed for the day of redemption. Let all bitterness and wrath and anger and clamor and slander be put away from you, along with all malice. And be kind to one another, tender-hearted, forgiving each other, just as God in Christ also has forgiven you.

—Ephesians 4:30-32

Others are watching! It really does matter what you do and how you live. Pursue character!

Keep your behavior excellent among the Gentiles, so that in the thing in which they slander you as evildoers, they may on account of your good deeds, as they observe them, glorify God in the day of visitation. —1 Peter 2:12

Now this I say, he who sows sparingly shall also reap sparingly; and he who sows bountifully shall also reap bountifully. —2 Corinthians 9:6

Along the Journey

Do you have any Do Not Disturb signs in areas of your life? Unlock all the "hidden" doors of your life and give God the keys. Remember, God is either Lord of all or not Lord at all!

What keys do you need to turn over to God, and what doors can He unlock with them?

_____

_____

God wants us to continually deepen our **dependence on Him.** The greater our dependence on Him, the less destructive we will be in our relationships with others. **"You shall love the Lord** your God with all your **heart,** and with all your **soul,** and with all your **mind."** This is the great and foremost commandment. And a second is like it, **"You shall love your neighbor as yourself."**

—Matthew 22:37–39

If someone were to make a thirty-second ad of your life, what current commercial would it be similar to?_____
_____
_____
_____
_____

Along the Journey

Respond **honestly,** and write the first thought that comes to your mind:
For me to live is
_____!

Is living anything but knowing Christ?

Paul realized that for him to live was knowing Christ. He compared everything else to rubbish. • More than that, I count all things to be loss in view of the surpassing value of knowing Christ Jesus my Lord, for whom I have suffered the loss of all things, and count them but rubbish in order that I may gain Christ. —Philippians 3:8

Remember, God is not a machine. He's the **King of kings!**
For the Lord Most High is to be feared, a great **King** over all the earth.

—Psalm 47:2

Eternal life is the life of God given to those who **by faith** know Jesus Christ as the leader of their lives and allow Him to control them.

We look not at the things which are seen, but at the things which are not seen; for the things which are seen are temporal, but the things which are not seen are eternal.

—2 Corinthians 4:18

All that I am and all that I can be are found in Jesus Christ.

If you could only sing one worship song for the rest of your life, what would it be?__

_____

_____

_____

_____

Be Thou exalted, O Lord, in Thy strength; we will sing and praise Thy power.

—Psalm 21:13

Catch a glimpse of
God's unconditional love

for you! Even when we do wrong, He loves us just the same.

And I pray that Christ will be more and more at home in your hearts, living within you as you trust in him. May your roots go down deep into the soil of God's marvelous love; and may you be able to feel and understand, as all God's children should, how long, how wide, how deep, and how high his love really is; and to experience this love for yourselves, though it is so great that you will never see the end of it or fully know or understand it. And so at last you will be filled up with God himself.

—Ephesians 3:17-19 LB

Remember,
_____,
(insert your name)

I am for you!

Who can be against you?

In all things, you are more than a **victorious** conqueror through Me. Be convinced that nothing can stop Me from loving you ...not death or life, angels or demons, current circumstances, or anything in your past or future. **Absolutely nothing** and no one in all of the entire world can separate you from My totally awesome, unconditional, and indescribable love for you!

—Romans 8:37–39, paraphrase

P.S. Remember, I will never leave or abandon you! Don't be afraid. I am your helper, and I'm with you every step of your journey.

—Hebrews 13:5–6, paraphrase

God made you to win!

God counsels us on how to be persuasive with our lives.

Behold, I send you out as sheep in the midst of wolves; therefore be shrewd as serpents, and innocent as doves.

—Matthew 10:16

along the journey

If someone were to follow you around for a day, what would they hear your life say about Jesus? _____

_____

_____

Father,
It's my desire to love You more than anyone or anything else. Remind me that nothing compares to You. Forgive me for the times when I have just honored You with words while my heart has been far away. Remind me that I'm just a branch and that it's not up to me to make things happen. Help me to remain with You and to bear fruit for You.

44

Believing in the Promises of God

Did you know that there are over eight hundred promises in the Bible? Each promise comes with a special invitation to know God personally and to take Him at His word for that promise. God's promises cover every facet of life from money to relationships to family life, peace, power, healing, protection, and guidance.

God promised Israel that He would lead them into the Promised Land. All they had to do was believe and obey. God told them to send twelve spies into the land to see what the land was like. This was God's way of telling them to investigate the promise. Anytime God gives you a promise, it always comes with an invitation to explore it.

But when the spies returned, ten of the twelve gave a bad report—they said the land was inhabited by giants. They didn't believe that God could bring them into the Promised Land. Joshua and Caleb, however, saw the same giants the other ten saw, but they trusted God. They responded out of faith, not out of fear. They chose to believe God for His promise. But the majority sided with the unbelieving spies, and because of their lack of faith, they wandered in the wilderness for forty years.

The promises of God are only promises until we take them off the pages of the Bible and plug them into our lives. The spies saw themselves as grasshoppers because they forgot that their help came from the Lord. The key to seeing God's promises come alive is faith! One of the principles of Scripture is: When God makes a promise—if we believe instead of doubt—then that promise will come to pass in our lives.

Step into His promises!

Do not be afraid any longer, only believe.
—Mark 5:36

Our entire **relationship** with God is built on how we respond to His **promises**. It's based on our response to God's Word.

God moves on the basis of His promises.
Every place on which the sole of your foot treads, I have given it to you, just as I spoke to Moses.
—Joshua 1:3

The Lord is for me; I will **not fear**; what can man do to me? —Psalm 118:6

Elements Found in All of God's Promises

1. **Potentials:**

What are the benefits of

2. **Problems:**

the promise in my life?

What will it cost me to

see this promise come

3. **Procedures:**

to pass in my life?

What will it take to

achieve the promise?

God can supply every unmet **need** in your life. The potential is unbelievable!

And my God shall supply all your needs according to His riches in glory in Christ Jesus. —Philippians 4:19

We respond to the promises of God either by fear or faith.

For you have not received a spirit of slavery leading to fear again, but you have received a spirit of adoption as sons by which we cry out, "Abba! Father!"

—Romans 8:15

It takes as much faith to live in fear as it does to believe that God will take care of your life and your needs. I sought the Lord, and He answered me, and delivered me from all my fears. —Psalm 34:4

THe bottom line of Christianity is that you do what you believe.

Along the Journey

What one promise in Scripture would you like to see come to pass in your life?_____
_____
_____
_____
_____.

For by these He has granted to us His precious and magnificent promises, in order that by them you might become partakers of the divine nature, having escaped the corruption that is in the world by lust. —2 Peter 1:4

FAITH is choosing to take God at His word, fully believing He will bring it to pass. And WITHOUT FAITH it is impossible to please Him, for he who comes to God must believe that He is, and that He is a rewarder of those who seek Him.
—Hebrews 11:6

Faith is the foundation of life.

Be faithful until death, and I will give you the crown of life.
—Revelation 2:10

49

Faith mixed with God's promises produces miracles.

Now faith is the assurance of things hoped for, the conviction of things not seen. —Hebrews 11:1

God wants us to **live by faith**—not fear, panic, or desperation. **"My life is in your hands."**

Have I not commanded you? Be strong and courageous! Do not tremble or be dismayed, for the Lord your God is with you wherever you go. —Joshua 1:9

If you could change one thing about your city, town, school, or home, what would it be?_____

_____

_____. Now begin to **pray about it!**

Looking upon them, Jesus said, "With men it is impossible, but not with God; for all things are possible with God."

—Mark 10:27

I can do all things **through** Him who **strengthens me.**

—Philippians 4:13

As you look at this promise, what are the potentials, problems, and procedures?
(See "Elements Found in God's Promises" on page 47.)

Potentials_____

Problems_____

Procedures_____

Father,

You know what I am currently facing. I ask that You would open my spiritual eyes to see the potential You have to work in this situation. I know You want the best for me and that You have a place for me in the big picture of Your purpose. Give me the spirit of Joshua and Caleb to trust You without doubting and to move forward with confidence that You will bring it to pass.

Accomplishing God's Will

Initially, God reveals Himself to us in broad terms: His moral will and His desire for us to know Him personally. As we begin to practice His general purpose for our lives, His specific purpose for each of us becomes clearer as we continue to walk with Him and interact with Him on a daily basis. The result is that we are refined into His will.

I've discovered that God reveals His purpose for our lives gradually—by allowing us to see only as far as we need to see at that time. As a flashlight illuminates only the path directly in front of us, so God will allow us to see far enough ahead to take one…more…step. When we obey Him up to that point, the light reveals the next step.

As Christians, we are called to a life of faith. God doesn't show us everything at once. He calls us to choose to take Him at His word, knowing that He is going to faithfully bring it to pass. It's impossible for us to please Him without this kind of step-taking faith. He wants us to trust Him to guide us each step of the way.

The great temptation for us is to rush ahead of the light that God has provided. The way we resist that temptation is by believing He knows our unique destination and has created a custom path just for us. Enjoy what He's doing in your life and keep moving toward Him—one step closer.

If you want to know what
These things I have spoken

God's will is for you, look in His
to you, that My joy may be in

Word. God's will is that you
you, and that your joy may be

know Him personally.
made full. —John 15:11

If you could accomplish only **one** thing during your lifetime, what would it be? _____

ChOOSe carefully!

See to it that no one takes you captive through philosophy and empty deception, according to the tradition of men, according to the elementary principles of the world, rather than according to Christ. For in Him all the fulness of Deity dwells in bodily form, and in Him you have been made complete, and He is the head over all rule and authority; —Colossians 2:8–10

God has a perfect agenda for your life. It is absolutely God's will that you be committed to what He has for you. Commit yourself to His agenda and live faithfully.

God's will is not a tight wire; it's a canyon. He gives us freedom to move.

It is impossible to know God's will without asking God.

And this is the confidence which we have before Him, that, if we ask anything according to His will, He hears us. —1 John 5:14

If God were to give you an answer to only one question, what would your

question be? _____

_____

_____

_____

Obedience is the standard for God's will. If I'm obedient, I am pleasing Him.

He who has My commandments and keeps them, he it is who loves Me; and he who loves Me shall be loved by My Father, and I will love him, and will disclose Myself to him. —John 14:21

To fulfill God's will is worth any sacrifice.

Now the God of peace, who brought up from the dead the great Shepherd of the sheep through the blood of the eternal covenant, even Jesus our Lord, equip you in every good thing to do His will, working in us that which is pleasing in His sight, through Jesus Christ, to whom be the glory forever and ever. Amen.

—Hebrews 13:20-21

If you could pass only one spiritual discipline on to your children, what would it be and why? _____

_____

_____

_____

If we could see God's will for our lives,

It's worth it to get to God's will.

The plans of the diligent lead surely to advantage, but everyone who is hasty comes surely to poverty.
—Proverbs 21:5

And the world is passing away, and also its lusts; but the one who does the will of God abides forever.
—1 John 2:17

Make a list of ways you can see God's will more clearly? _____

_____

_____

_____

we would PAY ANY PRICE to get it.

It comes through His Word

—you have to read it to know it.

How to Know When It's God's Will

Trust in the Lord with all your heart, and do not lean on your own understanding. In all your ways acknowledge Him, and He will make your paths straight.

—Proverbs 3:5–6

It calls for practice

— look out for distractions.

God creates a path for us
—we don't HAVE to MAKE it up.

It challenges passivity
—purpose blows us out of our routines.

It commands priorities
—our first priority is relationship with Him.

Anything God gives you permission to do will always come

The mind of man plans his way, but the

with a clear direction. We're either living with His

Lord directs his steps. —Proverbs 16:9

permission or without it.

Be confident that if God tells you something, He's also going to tell you how to do it. **As God guides, He provides.**

Many are the plans in

a man's heart, but

the counsel of the

Lord, it will stand.

—Proverbs 19:21

Therefore, we are

When you live a life fully

ambassadors for Christ, as

devoted to Christ, you are the

though God were

greatest argument for Jesus. But

entreating through us; we

the moment your focus turns

beg you on behalf of

toward yourself, you become the

Christ, be reconciled to

best argument against Jesus.

God. —2 Corinthians 5:20

God's will is not found, it's discerned. As you commit yourself to do what Scripture says the will of God is, His will for your life becomes clearer.

God's General Will for Your Life Is That You...

 Experience a real and living personal relationship with Jesus. (See 1 Timothy 2:3–4.)

 Rely on God's power by learning what it is to walk in His Spirit on a daily basis. (Read Ephesians 5:15–18.)

 Stay pure in your thoughts and relationships. (See 1 Thessalonians 4:3–7.)

 Do right by living a life of integrity. (Read 1 Peter 2:13–15.)

 Suffer for being right. (See 1 Peter 4:12–19.)

 Learn to say "Thank You" to God in all situations, knowing that God knows what will make you more like Him. (Meditate on Ephesians 5:20.)

The more committed you become to these six things, the easier it becomes to know God's will for your life. What one decision could you make today to help build these things in your life?

_____
_____
_____
_____
_____
_____

Choose to do the will of God in those areas!

Dear Jesus,

I confess the things that I've allowed to push you
out of first place in my life. Today, I choose to put
You first. I choose to identify with You in Your
sufferings and Your strength. Use the events
of my life to deepen my relationship with
You. I commit to pursue integrity in
the details and to be completely
Yours, even when no one else is
looking. The specifics of my
life are under Your control.
This day I will follow as
You lead.

CHAPTER 7

Renewing Your Mind

On the wall of a correctional center in Atlanta, a poem written in grease pencil caught my eye. The inscription read:

The Eagle and the Wolf
There's a battle between the eagle and the wolf.
The eagle inside of me represents everything that is
     good and pure.
And even though it soars through the valleys,
     it still lays its eggs on the mountain tops.
There's a wolf inside of me.
And the wolf preys upon my weaknesses
     and justifies itself in the presence of the pack.
Who will win the war between the eagle and the wolf?

There was a big space and then these words: **"The one that you feed."** I'll never forget the power of those words scrawled on that wall. Who wins the battle for your mind? The one you choose to feed. Who wins the battle for your life? The one you choose to build on. Who wins the battle between right and wrong? The one you choose to feed.

What thoughts are you feeding? Are you filling your life with God's truth, or are you feeding it a steady diet of TV, materialism, and out-of-control habits. It's easy to become desensitized and conformed to this world. But God calls us to be transformed by the renewing of our minds, to take every thought captive, and to be doers of the Word.

The key to
producing
lasting change
is renewing
our thought
life with God's
thoughts.

Do not be conformed to this world, but be transformed by the renewing of your mind, that you may prove what the will of God is, that which is good and acceptable and perfect. —Romans 12:2

Be devoted to things that are eternal!

1. The **person** of God
2. The **passions** of God
3. The **power** of God

If then you have been raised up with Christ, keep seeking the things above, where Christ is, seated at the right hand of God. Set your mind on the things above, not on the things that are on earth.

—Colossians 3:1–2

We have a condition that causes us to think, say, and feel things that are not true. Only God can change that condition.

Then I will sprinkle clean water on you, and you will be clean; I will cleanse you from all your filthiness and from all your idols.

—Ezekiel 36:25

Moreover, I will give you a new heart and put a new spirit within you; and I will remove the heart of stone from your flesh and give you a heart of flesh.

—Ezekiel 36:26

Photo By Greg Howell

And I will put My Spirit within you and cause you to walk in My statutes, and you will be careful to observe My ordinances.

—Ezekiel 36:27

What are three things that God says He'll do in any person who asks Him? (Found in Ezekiel 36:25–27)

1. _____
2. _____
3. _____

Anytime we listen strictly to our emotions, we will do the wrong thing.

For those who are according to the flesh set their minds on the things of the flesh, but those who are according to the Spirit, the things of the Spirit.

—Romans 8:5

In what situations are you most prone to be led by your emotions?

_____

_____

_____

_____

_____

God doesn't want us to be ruled by feelings. Instead, He calls us to be **ruled by faith.**

Teach me Thy way, O Lord; I will walk in Thy truth; unite my heart to fear Thy name.

—Psalm 86:11

Many of us are ruled by our hearts. Our feelings are real, but they're not always right. Our minds tend to justify what our hearts say.

The precepts of the Lord are right, rejoicing the heart; the commandment of the Lord is pure, enlightening the eyes.

—Psalm 19:8

66

One of the dangers of being single is that often there is no one to check up on you! So then each one of us shall give account of himself to God.

—Romans 14:12

You shall fear only the Lord your God; and you shall worship Him, and swear by His name.

—Deuteronomy 6:13

Warning

When faced with a decision that requires an action on your part, don't just settle for what's legal or moral or what you can get away with. Instead ask, is it holy??

We demolish arguments and every pretension that sets itself up against the knowledge of God, and we take captive every thought to make it obedient to Christ.

—2 Corinthians 10:5 NIV

If you could have one person on earth to disciple you, who would it be and why?_____
_____
_____
_____
_____
_____
_____

Photo By Greg Howell

Rule

your

How can a young man keep his way pure? By keeping it according to Thy word. Thy word I have treasured in my heart, that I may not sin against Thee. —Psalm 119:9, 11

instincts!

Be grounded in God's Word

Look up the topic you are struggling with in a concordance and write the applicable verses down on index cards. Place the cards around your house and in your car. Memorize scriptures that will help you with the areas where you are falling into temptation or sin.

68

Sold Out

Does God sit in and own every seat in the arena of your life? Is He Lord of your thought life, your relationships, your career, your schedule, and every decision of your life?

Father, I've been holding back some areas of my life from Your control. Become Lord of _____

Prayer

Search me, O God, and know my heart. Show me the things in my life that are stealing my joy by causing me to worry and fear. Help me to surrender every anxious thought to You. Replace my worry with Your supernatural peace. Reveal any hurtful ways in my life. Guide each thought and decision I make each step of the way.

See Psalm 139:23-24.

along the journey

What one thing ticks you off the most?_____

_____

_____

_____

Cease from anger, and forsake
wrath; fret not yourself, it leads
only to evildoing.

—Psalm 37:8

What one thing makes you the happiest? _____

_____

_____

_____

Finally, brethren, whatever is true, whatever is honorable,
whatever is right, whatever is pure, whatever is lovely, whatever is
of good repute, if there is any excellence and if anything worthy
of praise, let your mind dwell on these things.

—Philippians 4:8

Use this page to write out the dreams of your heart.
Write them as if they have already come to pass.

Watch over your heart with all
diligence, for from it flow the
springs of life. —Proverbs 4:23

Father,

Show me any areas of my life where I have exchanged Your truth for a lie and have let my feelings take me out of Your best for my life.

Remember that truth becomes subjective when we let our hearts control us instead of living by God's Word.

Being Power-Based

Your achievements are only as strong as the foundation on which they are built. There's a story in 2 Kings 4:1–6 that illustrates the need for being power-based. A woman goes to Elisha and says, "My husband has died and the creditors are after me. What shall I do?" Elisha tells her to go and borrow vessels from all of her neighbors. The vessels were miraculously filled with oil that she then sold to pay her debt.

The point of this story is that this woman had a community of believers she could go to with her need. The people of God were her power base.

So many people approach their relationship with God with the thought, "As long as I'm right with God, then I'm OK." Not so. Our lives are designed to be in community with other believers, because we need each other.

The truth of the story is that there is a dimension of God's power we cannot have in our lives without belonging to a community of believers. If you approach your life of faith alone, then your foundation is not complete and you are not working from a strong power base. You need a community of believers in your life.

Life is not about you doing things for God. It's about **allowing God** to do the things He wants to do through you!

God has looked down from heaven upon the sons of men, to see if there is anyone who understands, who seeks after God.
—Psalm 53:2

Christ Jesus Himself being the cornerstone, in whom the whole building, being fitted together is growing into a holy temple in the Lord; in whom you also are being built together into a dwelling of God in the Spirit.
—Ephesians 2:21–22

Without **God moving in us,** Christianity is just another club.

We all make our mistakes on our own, but nobody gets well alone. We need others.

Name a person who has helped you deal with a mistake you made.

_____.

Write about how they have helped you. _____

_____

_____

_____

_____

Is anyone among you suffering? Let him pray. Is anyone cheerful? Let him sing praises. Is anyone among you sick? Let him call for the elders of the church, and let them pray over him, anointing him with oil in the name of the Lord; and the prayer offered in faith will restore the one who is sick, and the Lord will raise him up, and if he has committed sins, they will be forgiven him. Therefore, confess your sins to one another, and pray for one another, so that you may be healed. The effective prayer of a righteous man can accomplish much. —James 5:13–16

Photo by Greg Howell

We often falsely think that the power of God changes according to how we experience it. But God is unchangeable! And for this purpose also I labor, striving according to His power, which mightily works within me. —Colossians 1:29

thought...

You may think you can commune with God in bed, while watching TV, or sitting by the lake. But I promise you, He's not there. He is in the body of believers.

Again I say to you, that if two of you agree When you are not rightly related to a on earth about anything that they may community of believers, it will affect the ask, it shall be done for them by My Father power of your prayer life. who is in heaven. —Matthew 18:19

Being power based means that we switch strengths. It is found when we STOP doing things on our own and begin to live out of God's unlimited power. The God who girds me with strength, and makes my way blameless.
—Psalm 18:32

There is no need that can't be met when believers come together. Our lives are to be locked into a community of believers.

God has so composed the body, giving more abundant honor to that member which lacked, that there should be no division in the body, but that the members should have the same care for one another. And if one member suffers, all the members suffer with it; if one member is honored, all the members rejoice with it.
—1 Corinthians 12:24-26

The church is the base from which you build your life and affect the world. If you could speak one time in front of your church, what would you say?_____
_____
_____
_____
_____

Photo by Greg Howell

Christianity is not a solo sport.

What is your greatest spiritual virtue?_____
_____
_____.

There's a church that needs it!

You will surely wear out, both yourself and these people who are with you, for the task is too heavy for you; you cannot do it alone. —Exodus 18:18

We've become a society of buffet believers, going from event to event, sampling God here and there, instead of finding a group of believers and committing to it.

We'll be blown away every time something happens or goes wrong if we are ruled strictly by our emotions, circumstances, and feelings.

the journey along

Does the power of God make you uncomfortable? Do you get close enough to Him to take notes and do the "Religious Thing," but not quite close enough to connect to His unlimited power source? Are you settling for mediocrity in your walk with Him???

Dear God,

When I look at my life from Your perspective, I see that the task is too big for me and that I need other believers in my life. During this season of my life, heighten my sensitivity to which church I could best function in with my gifts and needs. Create in me a desire to commit to that community of believers.

Waiting on God

Riding on an airport shuttle, I met a man with an unusual job; the job was equivalent to a military bounty hunter. He traveled around the country finding soldiers who had gone AWOL and brought them back to face military charges.

He said that a lot of young guys fresh out of high school sign up because their friends do or their parents pressure them to enlist or they think it will be "fun" to travel and make money. But then they find that they hate the discipline and all the rigorous physical demands of being in the military.

He pointed out that instead of waiting and going through all of the cumbersome paperwork, they often get frustrated and decide to take off. Numerous times he mentioned that if these soldiers were willing to wait, they could get out of duty without all of the negative consequences of being caught for desertion.

Some of us get into similar situations in the Christian life. We make an initial commitment to God, but we don't like it when God starts placing demands on our lifestyle and time. In a society of ATMs, microwaves, instantaneous e-mails, fast food, and FedEx, we don't like to wait when God slams the brakes on in our lives. Often we're faced with the temptation of going AWOL or wanting to rush ahead of God's will for us.

But as we are willing to wait, God refines us. He weeds out our tendencies to do our own things in our own strength and gives us His courage and strength. We benefit from His discipline, and He causes us to walk with a new and stronger dedication and confidence. During seasons of waiting, we say with our lives—not just our lips—"Jesus, You are truly Lord."

The problem is often that we are focusing on the immediate results. . .while God is focusing on His relationship with us!

But I have this against you, that you have left your first love. Remember therefore from where you have fallen, and repent and do the deeds you did at first; or else I am coming to you, and will remove your lampstand out of its place—unless you repent.

—Revelation 2:4-5

thought. . .

Is the favor of God present in your life? God is not duty bound to bless you if you run ahead of His plans for your life. Remember no one can do for you what God can do!

My soul, wait in silence for God only, for my hope is from Him. —Psalm 62:5

Often God restricts us in order to refine us. The call of God is always a call of preparation!

And let us not lose heart in doing good, for in due time we shall reap if we do not grow weary.
—Galatians 6:9

Indicators
Warning that it's wise to wait:

You are:
1. Frustrated—Psalm 94:19
2. Confused—James 1:5
3. Doubtful—Mark 11:22–23
4. Highly Emotional—Psalm 55:22
5. Desperate—Psalm 42:5–11
6. Revengeful—Proverbs 20:22
7. Judgmental—1 Corinthians 4:5

I am weary with my crying; my throat is parched; my eyes fail while I wait for my God.
—Psalm 69:3

Consequences
of not waiting for God's timing:
1. We hurt others.
2. We delay success.
3. We prolong the season of waiting.

If we hope to get through a season of standing or waiting, we're going to have to use the Word of God as a sword.

Sustain me according to
Thy word, that I may live;
and do not let me be
ashamed of my hope.

—Psalm 119:116

When expectations clash
with reality,
frustration results.

1. God's ways are **wisest!**

   Isaiah 40:28

2. God's timing is **best!**

   Ecclesiastes 3:1, 11

3. God's grace is **sufficient** for you!

   2 Corinthians 12:9

along the journey

Are you mistaking God's patience for His

permission? Just because you feel something

is right doesn't mean it is!

The only times you should never delay is when you give your life to Jesus and when you make peace with God.

Seek God as you wait. Write a prayer about your tendency to rush ahead. Let Him refine that tendency into strength and courage.

I waited patiently
for the Lord; and
He inclined to me,
and heard my cry.
—Psalm 40:1

The results of waiting:
- Jesus gets the credit.
- Friends get to see God at work in your life.
- You get to see the power of God.
- You get to see God pull off the impossible.
- Your enemies are destroyed.

Cease striving and know that I am God; I will be exalted among the nations, I will be exalted in the earth. —Psalm46:10

Waiting reaffirms God's promise. When God puts the brakes on in your life, He also delivers a promise.

I would have despaired unless I had believed that I would see the goodness of the Lord in the land of the living. Wait for the Lord; be strong, and let your heart take courage; yes, wait for the Lord. —Psalm 27:13–14

Waiting is remaining faithful until God gives **further instruction.**

Not that I have already obtained it, or have already become perfect, but I press on in order that I may lay hold of that for which also I was laid hold of by Christ Jesus.
—Philippians 3:12

By definition, waiting is not something quick. It's not sitting and doing nothing. Waiting isn't being careless. Waiting is trusting God and saying with my life, **"You are really Lord!"**

When you find yourself in less than desirable conditions, are you willing to stay there long enough for **God** to mature you and to **bring you through** it?

If you were going to run from God, what kind of shoes would you wear?

Read Luke 11:9–10. If you could paint a billboard that would tell people why they should wait on God, what would it say?

When you are in a season of waiting, it's easy to believe that the best days are behind you. God challenges you, "Will you believe it can be **good again**?" Do not say, "Why is it that the former days were better than these?" For it is not from wisdom that you ask about this.
—Ecclesiastes 7:10

For   many…are

enemies of the

Cross of Christ,

When you are overwhelmed
whose   end   is

and come to the end of
destruction,

yourself, picture the Cross...
whose god is

their appetite,

and whose glory

is in their shame,

who set their

minds on earthly

things.

—Philippians

3:18–19

But now in Christ Jesus you
who formerly were far off
have been brought near by the
blood of Christ.
—Ephesians 2:13

Don't settle for Mr. or
Miss Right Now!
Wait for God's
perfect Mr. or Ms.
Right for You.

"The Lord is my portion," says
my soul, "Therefore I have hope
in Him." The Lord is good to
those who wait for Him, to the
person who seeks Him.

—Lamentations 3:24–25

Father,

Help me to submit myself to Your agenda and Your timetable. Deepen my dependence on You and my hunger to know You. Help me discover Your joy and Your supernatural peace in the midst of waiting. I choose not to go AWOL. Give me Your courage and strength to hang in for the entire ride. Don't let me carelessly rush ahead of Your will. Help me to become more mature and complete through these difficult circumstances. Don't let me become bitter from the frustration...make me better. Thanks for loving me too much to leave me the way that I am.

CHAPTER 19

Making Good Choices—God Choices

All of life hinges on one word—choice. In that one word is the power to make life better and the ability to make life worse. Choice runs throughout every area of our lives.

- Relationships: "I thought it was true love."
- Work: "Will I always be standing behind the counter saying, 'Want fries with that?'"
- Finances: "Hey, money is no object if you don't have any."
- Emotions: "If it weren't for negative emotions, I'd have no emotions at all."
- Friendship: "With friends like these, who needs enemies?"

Let's face it, life is what you choose it to be. The difference between good choices and God choices is based on what you believe about the character of God.

- Will I choose to wait because I believe God is working things out?
- Will I choose to work as hard as I can to get the promotion because I believe God honors work?
- Will I choose to be responsible with my money because He is the owner and provider of all my wealth?
- Will I choose to open up the hurt and anger in my life because I believe He heals, as a loving and compassionate Father?
- Will I choose to deal with harmful friendships and pick healthy ones because I believe He is the model of a true friend?

You see, if you don't believe God is a good God, you won't make good choices. However, if you believe He is a rewarder of those who seek Him, your choices will be God's choices.

We all find ourselves at impasses where we have to make choices. When you do, you must ask W.D.G.W.—What Does God Want?

Decide on the results now! Make a decision to stick to what is right. Don't settle for anything less than God's best!

But examine everything carefully; hold fast to that which is good; abstain from every form of evil.
—1 Thessalonians 5:21–22

It's easy to settle for second best. God gives you the ability to make choices. When you make the choice, God makes the change!

For the Lord gives wisdom; from His mouth come knowledge and understanding. He stores up sound wisdom for the upright; He is a shield to those who walk in integrity, guarding the paths of justice, and He preserves the way of His godly ones. —Proverbs 2:6–8

Always land
on the side of **right**
in the details of your life!

Is not the whole land before you? Please
separate from me: if to the left, then I
will go to the right; or if to the right,
then I will go to the left. —Genesis 13:9

What area in your life would you say you are exactly
like God and why?_____

_____

_____

_____

You can't lose God's joy...but you can forfeit it by the choices you make! **Joy is a choice.**

This is the day which the Lord has made; let us rejoice and be glad in it.
—Psalm 118:24

is it holy?

i.i.h.???

Is the deciding question of your life, **"is it holy?"**

Is what I'm about to do going to push me **closer to God,** or will it pull me farther away from Him?

Stop the justifying games. Are **you** practicing **holiness** in the fear of God?

Examine how your choices impact the spiritual dimension in your life.

If you could change one thing in your life, what would it be?

_____
_____
_____
_____
_____

THE one great temptation is to think you'll be happier away from God. But He is the one who Holds your destiny and your future.

How does Jeremiah 29:1–14 help you see God more clearly?_____

_____
_____
_____
_____
_____
_____

The wisdom of the prudent is to understand his way, but the folly of fools is deceit. —Proverbs 14:8

When we allow compromise in our lives, we have everything to lose and nothing to gain.

in times of trouble, and those who know Thy name will put their trust in Thee; for Thou, O Lord, hast not forsaken those who seek Thee. —Psalm 9:9-10

The Lord also will be a stronghold for the oppressed, a stronghold

If you could make one choice that would make you a **stronger believer**, what would it be? Place your response on the rock.

Each time we choose to go on our own, we're stepping back, not forward.

Why is it so important to God that you be holy? Read 2 Corinthians 6:15–18.

What are the benefits of choosing God's wisdom? Read Proverbs 2:5–12.

Stern discipline is for him who forsakes the way; he who hates reproof will die.
—Proverbs 15:10

Father,

Give me the strength to make a deliberate choice to be Your person. Give me the courage to look at every area of my life and to ask, **"is it holy?"** Lord, help me to change the areas that don't meet up to Your holy standard. Help me say no to the things I need to say no to and yes to the things You want me to choose. Thank You for loving me enough to want Your best for me. Thank You for being patient with me.

Dreaming God's Dream

My father left us when I was only five. I knew him only as the "defendant" from the courtroom. It was just Mom and me to fend for ourselves. At the age of ten, I was five feet tall and two hundred ten pounds. Later, I was diagnosed with epilepsy, a severe learning disability, and dyslexia. Because of my learning disability, I didn't learn to read until I was in the eighth grade. Public speaking was out of the question, as I couldn't even read a report in front of my class without getting sick. The experts told my mom that I would never amount to anything and doubted that I would ever graduate from high school.

But looking back, I now realize that my environment was a divine set-up from God. Because I grew up without a dad, struggled through school, and suffered other painful trials, God was able to birth in me a vision and set me on my life mission of communicating the truth of God the best way I know how.

God stirred me to become something bigger than I thought I could be. None of the experts would have predicted that today I have the opportunity to speak to over 200,000 people a year, traveling over 110,000 miles. I'm so thankful that I heard and obeyed God's dream instead of listening to the dismal future others had forecast for my life.

We must be careful that we don't squash the breeding ground for God's vision, just because we don't like the environment He has placed us in. Realize that it's out of what you've been through that God is going to stir something unique in you. He's preparing you.

He's already placed His vision and dreams inside you. Vision is only found in relationship with Him. May you lay aside your plans and dream His dreams. Don't envy the dreams He's given others or try to live out the dreams others have for you. God, your Creator, has a dream custom tailored just for you. Trust your heavenly Father to take the hard things from your past and orchestrate them to work them together for your good—as you dream His dream. Don't forget, you were purposely created to live out God's dream.

God's vision empowers you to do something beyond yourself. His vision stretches you beyond your natural capabilities.

Now to him who is able to do immeasurably more than all we ask or imagine, according to his power that is at work within us. —Ephesians 3:20 NIV

If you could ask God to do one thing for you without regard to earthly limitations, what would it be? _____
_____
_____
_____
_____
_____

For Thou art my lamp, O Lord; and the Lord illumines my darkness.
—2 Samuel 22:29

Vision is born out of what stirs you up. The more clearly defined your vision is, the better it will be. Realize that God is not restricted by your background. Your experiences and your trials haven't been wasted. You grew up in a certain place, at a certain time, in a certain way, for a specific purpose.

For Thou art my lamp, O Lord; and the Lord illumines my darkness.
—2 Samuel 22:29

What would you like to discover about yourself that you thought was true but was actually false?_____

_____

_____

_____

_____

We have **two choices:** We can either live vainly or we can live by God's plan and vision. Are you **choosing God's** dream or something else?

thought

If you don't live under God's vision, you'll be working under someone else's vision.

Unless the Lord builds the house, they labor in vain who build it; unless the Lord guards the city, the watchman keeps awake in vain.
—Psalm 127:1

Read Jeremiah 1:4–10. Examine God's life **mission** for Jeremiah. How can you apply it to your life **mission?**

What has God designed you to do? God has a primary **mission** for you. You were designed for that **mission**. It's the broad statement for your life— it's the theme of your life. It's God's big snapshot picture for your life.

Examples of Primary Missions from Biblical Characters

- **Moses**—to take the children of Israel out of Egypt
- **Esther**—to keep her people from being killed
- **Paul**—to spread the gospel to new lands
- **King David**—to be God's man

As you begin to follow the big picture for your life that God has revealed to you, God will fill in the gaps. He will focus your **mission** as you step out in faith. The more you allow God to define the vision, the more successful it will be.

Write in one sentence what your life mission is. I am to _____

_____

_____.

Take a sheet of paper and divide it into two columns. On the left column list all the different roles you play in your life: daughter, son employee, girlfriend, friend, Sunday school teacher, volunteer, etc. On the right column write down what your primary mission is for each role that you play.

thought...

If all the people you know in your life could say the same thing about you, what would you want that one thing to be?_____

_____

_____

_____

_____

_____

_____

Vision is not found; it's discerned by God's Spirit.

And this is my prayer: that your love may abound more and more in knowledge and depth of insight, so that you may be able to discern what is best and may be pure and blameless until the day of Christ.

—Philippians 1:9–10 NIV

During prevailing moments in your life, God will stir you to do something that is greater than you are. **Are you paying attention to the moments when vision is born?**

Don't confuse your job with vision. Your job is your task not your vision.

If you could invent one thing to help improve the lives of other people, what would it be? _____

_____

_____

Following God's vision brings true fulfillment! Be full on rocking for God in the things that He shows you to do, and watch the awesome results! Delight yourself in the Lord; and He will give you the desires of your heart. Commit your way to the Lord, trust also in Him, and He will do it. And He will bring forth your righteousness as the light, and your judgment as the noonday.
    —Psalm 37:4–6

When you aren't living out your primary mission, you will be extremely frustrated. Find your uniqueness and live it out!

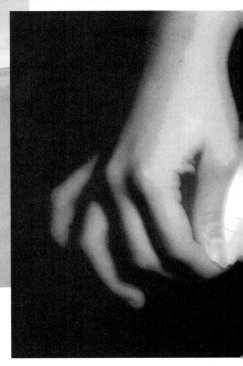

Why would believing that God is for you help you deal with the insecurities and worries that try to steal God's vision for you?

Photo by Greg Howell,

On a piece of paper list your worries, insecurities, and things that others have said that are holding you back from dreaming God's dream. Picture yourself giving that list to God. Release each fear individually to Him.

Burn or tear up the list as a symbol of placing it in God's hand. Feel the burden lifted.

_____,
(insert your name)
Cast all your cares on Me. Give Me the load
of your worries, doubts, and fears because I
deeply care for You!
—1 Peter 5:7 & Proverbs 20:24, paraphrases

Father, help me give all my dreams and worries to You. Let Your perfect peace guard my heart and my mind. Don't let the enemy paralyze me with the spirit of fear. Thank You that You have not given me a spirit of fear! Let Your perfect love drive out all fear that would try to stop me from being all that You created me to be!

If you could hear God audibly, what would you want Him to say to you?_____
_____

Maybe you'd hear Him say: "You aren't too old! You haven't missed My purpose! You haven't missed your moment! You haven't disqualified yourself by blowing it too many times!"

You are only **one step** away from God doing a fresh thing in your life!

For the vision is yet for the appointed time; it hastens toward the goal, and it will not fail. Though it tarries, wait for it; for it will certainly come, it will not delay.

—Habakkuk 2:3

Choose to dream His dream.

Lord,
Thanks that You already know the plans You
have for me. Make me sensitive to the prevailing
moments when You are stirring new things in my
life and are challenging me to do things
beyond myself. Help me to discover and
live out Your primary mission for my
life. Don't let me labor in vain. Give
me confidence to totally trust
You with my future, knowing
that You know my potential
better than I do. Father,
thanks for loving me
enough to walk with me
each step of the way and to
see me all of the way
through. In Your strong
and mighty name, Amen.

Write about how
your relationship
with God has made
you who you are.

_____

_____

_____

_____

_____

_____

_____

_____

_____

_____

_____

_____

_____

_____

Developing godly character requires taking on the things that God values. List your ten most important values. Then write about the life changes you need to make so that your values and your lifestyles will match.

_____

_____

_____

_____

_____

_____

_____

_____

_____

_____

_____

_____

_____

_____

God promises that if you call on Him, He will answer.
Close your eyes, ask Him for direction in a specific area
of your life. (Listen.) Open your eyes and begin to write.

_____

_____

_____

_____

_____

_____

_____

_____

_____

_____

_____

_____

_____

The Degree of forgiveness we extend to others determines the degree of forgiveness we receive. Write about what forgiveness means to you and what *not* forgiving is costing you.

_____

_____

_____

_____

_____

_____

_____

_____

_____

_____

_____

_____

_____

Life is a series of beginnings and endings. Write about the doors that are opening and closing in your life.

_____

_____

_____

_____

_____

_____

_____

_____

_____

_____

_____

_____

_____

DESTIN

PRINCIPLES FOR MAKIN

Destination speaks to young adults turned off by traditional programming and outreach. If you're concerned that your church may be losing a generation, here's a resource to help you do something about it.

- **1** — **Video 1: The Road Ahead**-David describes the places God wants to take young adults to make them more like Him. 0767326636

- **2** — **Video 2: Signs That You Don't Get It**-David points out some of the signs to look for—ways to know you've lost sight of the destination—and how to get back on track! 0767326644

- **3** — **Video 3: Enjoy the Ride**-David describes five positive reasons for trusting God in the details of life. 0767326652

- **4** — **Video 4: Getting to Your Destination**-David explains how asking the question "Is it holy?" helps Gen-Xers know and do God's will in any situation. 0767326660

  Each video is $19.95.

A booklet that explains in step-by-step form how to have a **relationship** with Jesus Christ. Great to use one on one or in large groups.

To **schedule** Dave to speak at your church, conference, or other event or to order tracts or tapes, **call** or **write:**

David Edwards Production, Inc.
P.O. Box 21504
Oklahoma City, OK 73156
405-840-3035
FAX 405-840-5785